Sew Your Own Accessories

Sew Your Own Accessories

~

By Joellen Sommer

With Elyse Sommer

Illustrated by Sherry Streeter

Lothrop, Lee & Shepard Co.
New York

Library of Congress Cataloging in Publication Data

Sommer, Joellen.
  Sew your own accessories.

  SUMMARY: Lists materials and gives instructions for
sewing a variety of accessories including belts, jewelry,
wallets, sewing kits, and handbags.
  1. Sewing—Juvenile literature. 2. Dress accessories—
Juvenile literature. [1. Sewing]
I. Sommer, Elyse. II. Streeter, Sherry, illus.
III. Title.
TT712.S65   646.4'8   72-1103
ISBN 0-688-40005-1
ISBN 0-688-50005-6 (lib. bdg.)

To my father . . . the best ever!

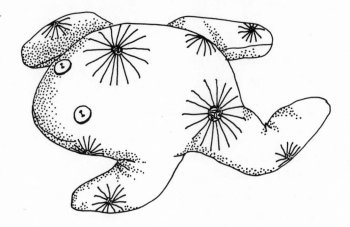

Contents

Books by Elyse Sommer

The Bread Dough Craft Book

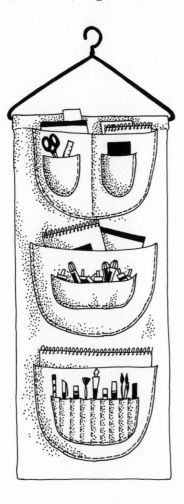

Introduction

Accessories are the little things that make a big difference!

Many fashion models keep an assortment of belts, scarves, and jewelry in their bags, to help them show clothes to their best advantage. At fashion shows, a specially trained person known as a fashion coordinator usually gathers accessories to complement the clothes to be shown.

These experts know one of the most important rules of fashion: no matter how well designed and beautiful an outfit is, accessories complete it and suggest individuality. Like fashion models and coordinators, interior designers know the importance of accessories to complete the look of a room. Just as a belt or a bag complements an outfit, so a throw pillow or a hanging completes and personalizes a room.

Sewing your own accessories is a wonderful way to develop an eye for fashion details, both in the things you wear and those you use. Knowledge of a few basic stitches and sewing techniques is all you need to complete the projects in this book. You can use almost any material, but the least expensive, such as denim and sailcloth, are often perfect. Since accessories require only small amounts of fabric, you can take advantage of bargains in remnant sales. In many instances, you can "recycle" old, otherwise unusable, fabrics into your sewing projects, to conform with our new understanding of ecology. Old coats, upholstery, and slipcovers can provide the basis for many sturdy and attractive accessories.

The sewing projects in this book are designed so that beginners can master them easily. These basic sewing techniques will permit you to go on to making complete outfits as your interest and ability develop.

If you have access to a sewing machine and know someone who can show you how to operate it, you can make the projects by machine, or use a combination of machine and handstitching. However, the projects can be made in a short time with or without a machine.

While sewing has been traditionally considered a "girls'" craft, more and more boys are becoming interested in sewing and designing. Many men have discovered the usefulness of handbags. Certainly, accessories like belts, book carriers, wallets, and room hangings have a unisex appeal. Boys browsing through this book who feel that sewing is strictly for girls should remember that many of our most important clothing and interior designers are men.

So, *everybody*, happy sewing!

Get Your Sewing Tools Together

NEEDLES—Use small-eyed fine needles when working with lightweight fabrics like cotton; heavier, larger-eyed needles when working with heavier, stiffer fabrics, such as denim and felt. A good rule is to use a needle with an eye just large enough to pull the thread through. A packet of needles in assorted lengths and eye sizes should fill all your sewing needs.

THREAD—With few exceptions, double-duty, or button, thread is ideal for sewing accessories. It is strong, threads easily into most needles, and does not have to be doubled. For lightweight materials, use plain mercerized cotton or silk thread. Whenever your stitches will show, use embroidery thread and needles.

SCISSORS—You will need one large pair of sharp scissors to cut fabric and a small pair of embroidery scissors to cut threads. Very handy scissors are pinking shears. These are large scissors that cut fabric with a zig-zag edge, which won't unravel. They're great for cutting large remnants into patches.

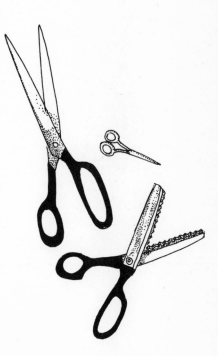

TAPE MEASURE OR RULER—Measure fabric with a cloth or metal tape measure or an eighteen inch ruler. While you should freely vary the shapes and decorative finishes suggested for the projects in the book, don't feel that omitting careful measuring is a step towards creativity. Have your tape or ruler on hand at all times to measure and remeasure. "Look before you leap" might well be changed to "Measure before you cut."

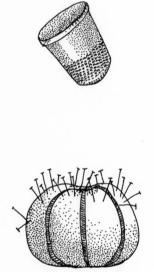

THIMBLE—Many consider the thimble essential to avoid sore fingers. Others feel more comfortable without one. This is such an inexpensive item that you can experiment to see whether you prefer to sew with or without it. If you do buy one, get one made out of metal, and be sure it fits your middle finger.

STRAIGHT PINS—Have lots of pins handy on a pincushion or in a covered box. Pin everything you can before you start to sew. Remove the pins as you work. Careful pinning can save basting or temporary stitching.

Stitches and Techniques

Once you master the stitches and techniques described in this section, you will be able to make all the accessories included, and more. If you decide to go on with your sewing and learn to make a complete wardrobe, you will have a good base from which to grow and learn.

Directions for making the various stitches, information about handling closings and decorations, and so on, will not be repeated with each project. Refer to your first project, The Sampler Bookmark, for the different stitches.

THREADING A NEEDLE—Use thread no longer than the length of your arm. Push one end of the thread through the eye of the needle and make a knot at the other end, so that the thread won't slip through the fabric when you begin to sew.

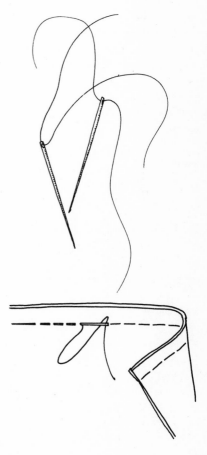

RUNNING STITCH—Make very small stitches of equal length (about ⅛ of an inch long) by passing the needle in and out of the fabric several times. Hold the fabric firmly between your left thumb and forefinger as you work.

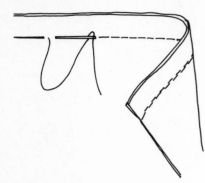

BACKSTITCH—This is the stitch you will be using more than any other to make the projects in this book. A very strong stitch, it is the same as the basic stitch made by a sewing machine. Here are two ways to make a backstitch:

1. Take two running stitches and then insert the needle into the material at the beginning of the last stitch. You will be one stitch ahead.

2. Make very small running stitches to the end of the two pieces you are joining. Make another row of running stitches at the same level as the first row, but let the stitches fill in the blanks.

STARTING AND STOPPING—A knot at the end of the thread when the needle is threaded is the most common method used to secure the first stitch. Instead of making a knot, you can take several small backstitches, one on top of the other, before starting to sew. To finish off, you can again make a knot by taking a backstitch and pulling your needle through the stitch before pulling it tight. However, three little backstitches, one on top of the other, are considered a neater way to wind off.

Always cut your thread with scissors. Don't tear it or bite it with your teeth. It is bad for your teeth and tends to rip your stitches and fabric!

HEMSTITCH—A hem hides raw edges, prevents unraveling, and holds a folded edge in place. First, fold over the raw edge very narrowly. Fold this over a second time so that it is about a ½ inch wide. Pin in place and press down the crease with your finger. Now make a small slanted stitch, inserting the needle so that it just catches hold of the main fabric; then pass the needle through the edge of folded fabric. The idea is not to have the stitches show on the right side.

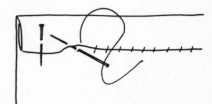

OVERHAND, OR OVERLAP, STITCH—This stitch joins two folded edges without a seam. Pin edges first so that they are sewn evenly. The overhand stitch should again be small (⅛ inch). Place the needle at right angles to the fabric and pull it through both folded edges. Repeat this procedure, keeping stitches close together. Don't pull the thread tight.

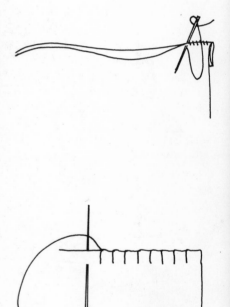

BLANKET STITCH—This is similar to the overhand stitch, but more decorative. When joining two pieces of fabric together on the right side with your joining stitch showing, use the blanket stitch. Make the same ⅛ inch stitch at the edge of the fabric, but straight up and down, instead of slanted. Before pulling the thread tight, weave the needle under the loop.

DECORATING WITH EMBROIDERY STITCHES— Sewing stitches are functional. Embroidery stitches are decorative. The blanket stitch, which is pretty enough to show on

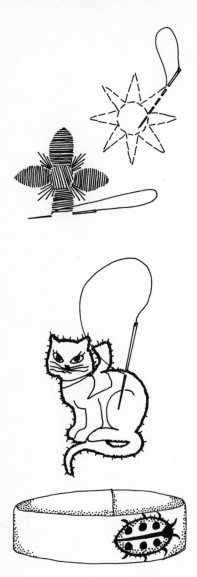

the right side of whatever you are sewing, is usually described as the first embroidery stitch.

There are many, many different kinds of embroidery stitches. Embroidery is a craft in itself. For the projects in this book you can embroider with the stitches described so far. Use embroidery thread instead of sewing thread (and, of course, embroidery needles), and make larger stitches. You can embroider initials, simple flowers, and designs with running, overhand, and backstitches. Blanket stitches will give any edge a decorative touch.

DECORATING WITH READY-MADE APPLIQUES —Embroidered appliques of all shapes, sizes, and colors are available in all sorts of stores. If you buy them singly in gift and variety stores, they can be quite costly. Browse through notions and trimming stores and try to buy them in packets of assorted sizes and shapes, or by the yard. Look through discarded clothing; remove appliques and reuse them.

DECORATING WITH HANDMADE APPLIQUES— Making your own appliques can be lots of fun and is very creative. The easiest way to create appliques is to cut the shapes you want out of felt. Raw edges will not have to be tucked in, and appliques can be glued or stitched in place. Felt cuts as easily as paper.

To create an applique out of a printed fabric:

1. Cut around the design with embroidery scissors, leaving a small rim around the design.

2. Pin the applique where you want to attach it.

3. Use embroidery thread and stitch the applique in place with overhand or blanket stitches, covering the small rim.

You can make appliques out of a solid, closely woven fabric. Instead of cutting out a printed design, use a felt-tipped waterproof pen to draw your own design on the fabric. Cut and sew as you would a printed applique.

DECORATING WITH TRIMMINGS—As you wander through the notions section of your local stores you will discover many useful trimming items to help you add special touches to accessories.

Ball fringes, tassel fringes, and rope fringes are available in all types of fabrics and luscious colors.

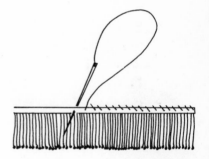

Edgings of lace or metallic fabrics, or cloth encrusted with tiny jewels are available in inexpensive packets and can be used to decorate accessories. You will find lots of "reusables" on discarded clothing too!

Sew trimmings to your accessories with small overhand stitches. Some are available in glue-on versions, but you usually pay extra for this convenience, and stitches tend to hold better.

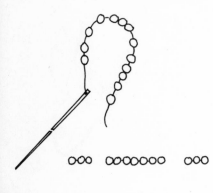

DECORATING WITH BEADS—Beaded decorations have been popular for centuries. Use anything from wooden beads to large glitter beads, to decorate a collar or belt. Hobby and notions shops can supply you with an untold variety. You may have enough discarded beads around your house to fill all your beading needs.

The best way to attach beads to fabric is to string them as you would a necklace. Mark out a pattern for the beads on the fabric with a fine pencil line (if you have tailor's chalk, use that) and sew the beads in place with overhand stitches between every second or third bead.

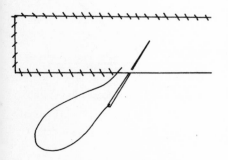

RIBBONS—Ribbons are available in every conceivable type of material, from simple grosgrain to elaborate tapestry ribbons. Narrow ribbons can be used to make striped decorations. Wide ribbons can serve as the main material for belts, suspenders, headbands, necklaces, or handsome handbag handles.

Since ribbons serve as both fabric and trimming, become a ribbon collector. Flea markets and church bazaars often sell end pieces or rolls of ribbons at savings.

BUTTONS—Buttons also serve a very important function in creating original accessories. You can close a bag or belt with a button-and-loop closing, and you can use buttons decoratively in place of, or in addition to, the other decorating techniques mentioned. For example, two large buttons can make eyes for a stuffed-animal pillow; small shirt buttons can be used to make a monogram or small flower. Tiny fabric emblems can be glued to buttons to give three-dimensional embroidered effects. Buttons can be arranged to form stripes and other patterns.

With all the accessory uses for buttons, it is important to learn to sew them on properly:

1. Put the needle into the fabric from the bottom and bring it up through a buttonhole.

2. Put the needle through the opposite hole and pull the thread through.

3. Repeat this procedure until your thread has gone through each buttonhole three or four times. If you are sewing on a button with four buttonholes, sew through the second set of buttonholes as you did the first.

4. When you are ready to wind off, bring the needle from the top of the button through the hole, but not through to the bottom of the fabric. Wind the thread around underneath the button at least five times and then bring your needle through the back. Wind off with three back stitches.

Some buttons are made with one toggle hole on the underside. In this case pass your thread through the toggle hole and back through the fabric until the button is securely attached.

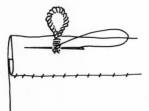

LOOPS—Ready-made loops are available in many sizes and fabrics. Frog loops are attractive.

There are several ways to make loops:

1. Use a sturdy, decorative rayon twill cord and cut into 4 or 5 inch lengths, depending upon the size of the loop needed. Twist the ends of the loop together and sew them to the underside of your fabric with small, close overhand stitches, as illustrated.

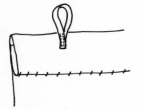

2. Cut narrow ribbons or pieces of felt into 4 or 5 inch lengths. Bring one end up over the other, as shown in the sketch, and attach with one or two rows of backstitches.

3. Thread your needle with doubled button thread. Sew three double lengths (the size of the loop you want) to each side of your fabric. Now wind your thread crosswise until the loop is tightly wound together.

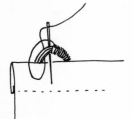

ZIPPERS—Zippers are available in a wide assortment of colors and sizes. When making accessories you will be using zippers mostly for bags with large openings.

To attach a zipper:

1. Measure your opening carefully and

get the right size zipper to fit the opening.

2. Turn the material to which the zipper will be attached inside out.

3. Turn the closed zipper face down.

4. Pin the tape edge of the zipper to one side of the fabric. If the fabric has a raw edge, it must be tucked and pinned under with the zipper tape. Baste the portion you have pinned with very loose running stitches. Once you become more experienced, you can skip the basting.

5. Open the zipper and pin the other side to the opposite fabric edge. Baste with loose running stitches.

6. Sew the zipper on with a backstitch.

VELCRO—An even more modern and easier type of closing than a zipper is Velcro. This consists of two pieces of tape that lock together when they are pressed between the fingers. They pull apart with a flick of the forefinger. This material is not as widely used in sewing as zippers because it is still expensive. However, a yard of Velcro can be used for many accessories and is more flexible than a zipper. A tiny purse opening or a necklace or headband closing, for example, would require an inch or two of Velcro. Sew Velcro in place with backstitches. It can be glued in place but if you plan to wash the article you are making, sewing is recommended. Substitute Velcro wherever you might use buttons, hooks and eyes, or snaps.

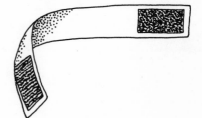

HOOKS AND EYES—You will be using hooks and eyes mostly for closing headbands, chokers, and possibly for belts. Always sew hooks and eyes with button-strength or doubled thread. Use small overhand stitches, as shown in the sketch.

Snaps are attached and used in the same manner as hooks and eyes.

HEM OR SEAM ALLOWANCE—When cutting out a pattern of any material except felt, always allow at least ⅝ of an inch all around for tucking and sewing under the fabric so that it won't fray. If you use pinking shears to cut your fabric and it is closely woven, the tucked-under fabric need not be basted before the sides are attached.

CASINGS—A casing is a pocket or tube through which to pull a ribbon or elastic; for example, a ribbon handle for a draw-string bag.

To make a casing:

1. Tuck and fold over ¼ inch of fabric and press it flat with your fingers.

2. Fold over another layer of fabric, wide enough for the pull-through material, and pin it in place.

3. Sew with backstitch or hemstitch.

4. To pull ribbon or elastic through a casing, pin down one end and attach a large safety pin to the other. Pull the safety pin through the casing.

SEWING FABRICS TOGETHER—Whenever two pieces of fabric are sewn together, the right sides should face each other. Every fabric except felt has a right and a wrong side. The right side is the side that shows when an article is finished. When you sew two pieces of fabric together, make sure the right side of each faces the other. Sew them on the underside or the wrong side. When you are finished turn the item right-side out.

IRONING—For a really professional look always press your fabric before you start cutting and sewing. Press it again when the project is finished, giving special care to stitched seams. In some projects where joined seams will be covered up before you are finished (for example, the patchwork belt), press open the seam as soon as it is sewn. Open the seam either with your fingertip or the tip of your iron.

Most fabrics are pressed on the wrong side to avoid a sheen. Polished cottons and chintzes are pressed on the right side to preserve their sheen. If you don't have a steam iron, put a damp cloth over the material you are pressing.

Sampler Bookmark

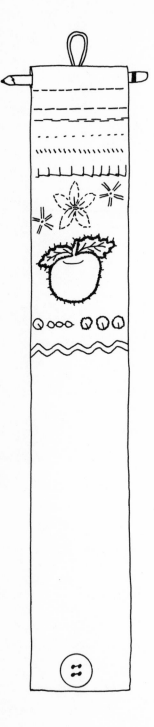

Making this bookmark will give you an opportunity to practice all the stitches and techniques just described. The hook and button closing will enable you to button the bookmark around this reference section. The top casing will hold a pencil for jotting down your own accessory ideas.

Materials:

two lengths of fabric, 3 by 23 inches, one
    solid colored and one printed
buttons, appliques, rickrack, and so on
felt, ribbon, or cord

How to Make It:

1. Starting two inches from the top of the solid-colored fabric, decorate an 8 inch length with a sampling of stitches and applique techniques. Make a row each of running stitches, backstitches, hem stitches, overhand stitches, and blanket stitches. Stitch in your initials, a daisy, or a small bug with one or a combination of stitches. Sew on a ready-made applique and then one made out of a printed fabric. Fill in the rest of the space with some button and bead trims.

2. Pin the solid and print fabrics together on both 23 inch edges and one 3 inch edge, with the right sides facing each other. Sew the edges together with backstitches.

3. Turn the bookmark right-side out, using

a thin stick or pencil to push it through.
4. Make a ¾ inch casing at the open end of the bookmark, and sew a hook to the underside of this casing.
5. Sew a button large enough to fit the loop to the other end of the bookmark.

You can outline the edges of the bookmark with decorative blanket stitches or rickrack. Steps 2, 3, and 4 can be eliminated if you use a single piece of felt.

Belts, Belts, Belts

Ribbon Belt

You can have a whole wardrobe of handsome belts. Start with a handmade ribbon belt, which requires a minimum of sewing and gives maximum wear.

Materials:

embroidery ribbon, 1½ to 2 inches wide.
　To determine the amount you need, measure your waist or hips, depending on where you wear your belts, and add 4 inches to this. For instance, if your waist is 22 inches, you will need a 26 inch ribbon to make a waist belt
one set of metal belt loops

How to Make It:

1. Place the ribbon with the right side against your working surface and sew down the raw edges at each end with hemstitches.
2. Slip one end of the ribbon through both belt loops and sew it down with backstitches. Make three rows of stitches to be sure the loops are secure.
3. If your ribbon is a solid color, decorate it with trimming or embroidery detail.
　If you use a lightweight ribbon, like

grosgrain, it is best to use two lengths doubled up. Sew the ribbons together on each side with the right sides facing out. Sew with matching or contrasting-colored thread, using backstitches, which will serve as a decorative border.

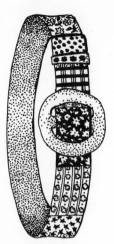

Patchwork Belt

Patching small pieces of material together to make an attractive item is an old form of stitchery art. Patchwork designs are especially suitable for belts. Don't be afraid to mix colors and designs. That's the fun of it all!

Materials:

printed cotton squares, 4 by 4 inches. Eleven patches will make a belt for waistlines up to 28 inches wide

solid-colored backing fabric, 4 by 50 inches (the backing for the illustrated belt was made from the leg of an old pair of lightweight men's trousers)

round or square buckle with a 4 inch opening

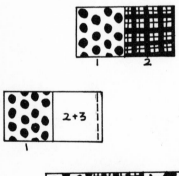

How to Make It:

1. Put the right sides of two patches together and sew them on one side with a backstitch. Unfold the sewn-together patches and press open the seams. (You can do this when all your patches are sewn.)

2. Sew the third patch to the second, as illustrated. Unfold, and repeat with a fourth patch, and a fifth, and so on, until all the patches are sewn together.

3. Sew down the raw edges along the length of patchwork and the solid-colored backing fabric.

4. Pin the patchwork and the solid fabric with their right sides together. Pin all but one 4 inch end. Sew the other three sides together with backstitches. Turn the belt right-side out through the open end, and close it with overhand stitches.

5. With the patchwork side facing you, pull one end of the belt through the first buckle opening, then over the bar and down through the second opening. Fold down a 3 inch length of the belt, and sew it down with hemming or overhand stitches.

6. Make a loop from a 1½ by 6 inch strip of printed fabric. Sew down the raw edges and fold the loop in half so it fits around the width of the belt. Tack the loop down at the back with three rows of backstitches.

If you don't have a buckle, cut the rim from a 5 inch plastic container lid. Cut two openings, as shown in the sketch. Paint the buckle with two coats of acrylic or latex paint; or cut fabric to fit the face of the buckle and glue it down. Coat this with two or three layers of varnish or lacquer. If you'd rather not use a buckle, you can wear your belt as a tie belt. This would eliminate the need to make a loop.

Cinch Belt

A cinch to make, this belt is a cinch to draw a flurry of compliments! Velvet ribbons will make it truly elegant. The belt illustrated was made in soft blue and yellow velvet with blue loops and a yellow drawstring.

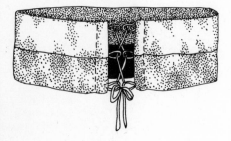

Materials:

two 2 inch wide ribbons. Measure your waist and add ¾ of an inch to get the amount you need

one 6 inch piece of twill cord to match one of the ribbons

one 18 inch piece of twill cord to match the other ribbon

How to Make It:

1. Place the ribbons together with the right sides facing each other, and sew them together with backstitches.
2. Sew down the raw edges at each end.
3. Cut the shorter piece of twill into six 1 inch lengths. Sew three loops of twill to each end of the belt.
4. Weave the long twill cord through the loops, like a shoelace.

If you plan to make a number of these belts for gifts or to sell, or if you like the idea of a lace-up closing on pants and skirts, you might want to invest in an eyelet plier, which helps you to put eyelet holes into fabric. It works like a hole puncher. This low-cost refillable plier is available with refills at notions stores.

Felt Link Belt

Since this belt is made with many small pieces use felt, which has no raw edges to sew down. Soft leather is also suitable, but it is more difficult to stitch.

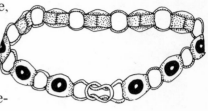

Materials:

ten gold 1 inch curtain rings (or more, depending upon size of your waist or hips)

looped gold belt closing (the illustrated buckle is available in all notions stores)

eleven pieces of felt, 1½ x 3 inches (more pieces if you use more rings), plus bits of felt in contrasting colors

How to Make It:

1. Cut the felt squares narrow enough to fit through the loops (see sketch).

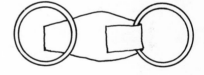

2. Cut smaller shapes from the contrasting-colored felt and sew one to the center of each felt piece, like flower centers. The illustrated belt was done in a patriotic motif, with Navy blue felt loops and white and red trims. Buttons or beads, instead of felt bits, can be sewn to the loops.

3. Bring the ends of each felt loop through a ring and pin them together at the back. Repeat this until all the metal and felt loops are attached. Each end loop will be sewn to a closing piece.

4. Sew each felt loop down firmly with a double row of backstitches.

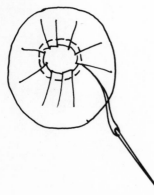

inside

Fabric-Rosette Belt

Our great-grandmothers used to make entire quilts out of fabric rosettes. Wearing rosettes around your waist or hips would be a fun way to give an old art a new look.

Materials:

4 inch squares of fabric: enough to fit around your waist or hips, and eight extra squares so that you can tie the ends and let them hang. Use a soft fabric so thread will pull through it easily. Mix or match solids and prints

How to Make It:

1. Use a 4 inch diameter cardboard circle as a template and cut out fabric circles.
2. With the wrong side of the fabric towards you, tuck down the raw edges, making a ½ inch crease.
3. Make a running stitch along this tucked-down edge and pull the thread as you go. When you have circled the fabric, bring your needle around the right side of the fabric and pull the thread as you would a drawstring. Your circle will look like a little puff, or a rosette. Wind off the thread and flatten the rosette.
4. When you have enough rosettes, sew them together at each side with small overhand stitches.

Belt-Looper Purse

A purse to loop around a belt is both good looking and practical. The two buttons make it adjustable to belts of any width.

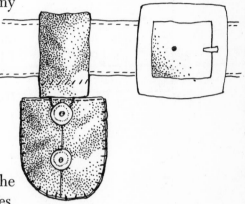

Materials:

felt, 3½ by 7 inches
decorative ribbon, 2 by 7 inches
two buttons

How to Make It:

1. Fold the felt in half lengthwise. Cut the folded ends, giving them rounded shapes, and save the scraps for decorative trims and a loop.

2. With embroidery wool sew three sides of the purse (see sketch) with blanket stitches.

3. Sew down the raw edges at each end of the ribbon. Sew one end of the ribbon to the inside top of the purse back, and sew the other end to the felt loop.

4. Sew buttons to the front of the purse and loop the ribbon around either of these, depending on width of the belt you are wearing.

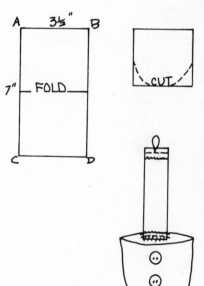

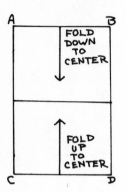

Belt-Looper Tissue Holder

You'll never hunt for a tissue with this case looped to your belt.

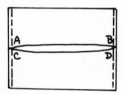

Materials:
fabric, 6 by 14 inches
1 inch wide grosgrain ribbon

How to Make It:
1. Fold the fabric into a 6 by 7 inch piece with the right sides facing each other, and sew. Leave a 2 or 3 inch opening.
2. Turn fabric right-side out and close the opening. You now have a doubled piece of fabric.
3. Fold sides AB and CD to meet at the center, as shown in the diagram.
4. Sew them in place as shown in the diagram. Turn the pockets inside out.
5. Cut two pieces of ribbon for loops to fit around your favorite belt. Sew them to the back of the tissue holder with two or three rows of backstitches.

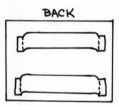

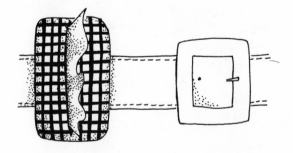

Scarf Belt

A scarf belt leads a dozen lives. Fold it
in half lengthwise and wear it as a sash.
Fold it twice over and pull it through your
pants' loops, like a ribbon belt. Tie it
around your head for an Appache Indian
sash, or tuck it into a V-necked dress or
blouse as an ascot.

Materials:

fabric, 8 by 46 inches. If you have a very
   long, wide strip of fabric, you can cut off
   an 8 inch width for this scarf belt and
   save the rest for the all-purpose skinny
   tie (see "For the Top of Your Head" in
   Contents)

How to Make It:

1. Cut the ends at an angle.
2. Fold down and sew all the raw edges
with small hemstitches.

Skinny Suspenders

Who said suspenders have an old-fashioned look? All your friends will want to know how to make them when they see the suspenders you've made out of bright upholstery ribbons or decorative elastic.

Materials:

2 yards of sturdy upholstery ribbon or decorative elastic, 1 inch wide

one set of mitten grippers. The findings used for commercially made suspenders are available if you search for them. However, they are usually expensive; and mitten grippers, available in any variety store, are just as good

two 2 inch pieces of Velcro

How to Make It:

1. Cut the ribbon in half and sew down the raw edges at each end.

2. Pull 2 inches of the ribbon through the opening of one gripper and sew the end down with small overhand stitches. Repeat this with the other ribbon.

3. Clamp the grippers with the sewn ribbon to the back of your pants. (You might get someone to help you with this step, for the best possible fit.) Crisscross the ribbons at the highest part of your back. Stitch down the portions where the ribbons cross with several rows of back-stitches.

4. Pull the front ends of your suspenders through the other gripper closings. Instead of sewing these down, sew a piece of Velcro to each suspender strap so that it will open and close and be adjustable. The Velcro can be 2 inches long or longer if desired.

Wide Notebook-Ring Suspenders

Once you start wearing suspenders, you'll want wide ones as well as skinny ones. Again, the findings are difficult to find and expensive. The secret: notebook rings to hook to your pants loops.

Materials:

2 yards of very wide upholstery ribbon or decorative elastic

four notebook-binder rings, large enough to fit around your suspenders. These open and close with a press of your fingers

two 2 inch pieces of Velcro

How to Make It:

1. Follow the directions for the skinny suspenders in the preceding project. Instead of pulling the ribbon ends through the mitten grippers, you will be using notebook rings that open and close.

2. To wear your suspenders, just hook the rings through the loops of your pants.

For the Top of Your Head

Floppy Hat

A big floppy hat is always fun to wear in the summer for protection from the sun, or in the winter for warmth. Make these hats in cool cottons and warm flannels and knits.

Materials:
½ yard fabric
1 inch wide elastic, long enough to fit around your head
bias tape, as long as the elastic

How to Make It:
1. Make a newspaper pattern similar to the sketched pattern. Side A of your pattern should be 8 inches, Side B should measure 22 inches, and the height, Sides C, should measure 13 inches.
2. Cut two pieces of fabric, using the paper pattern. Pin them together, with the right sides facing each other. Then sew them together with backstitches, at the sides (C). There will be a circular opening for the top and bottom of the hat.
3. Cut a 6 inch diameter circle out of

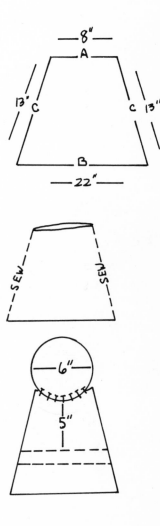

newspaper, and a piece of fabric from this pattern.

4. Pin the narrow end of the hat to the edges of the fabric circle. Make a few tucks as you pin to make the hat fit the circle.

5. Pin bias tape around the hat, starting 5 inches below the crown of the hat. This should leave a 3 inch brim. The bias tape is a casing for the elastic. Sew it down at the top and bottom with backstitches but leave an opening so that you can insert and pull through the elastic.

6. Pin down one end of the elastic. Pin a safety pin to the other end. Hold on to this safety pin and pull the elastic through the bias tape. Pin the elastic down but don't sew it yet. Try on the hat to see if it fits. If the hat is too loose, cut off a piece of the elastic. If it's too tight, add a piece of elastic or use a longer piece. When you are satisfied with the fit, sew down the ends of the elastic with backstitches.

7. Sew down the raw edges of the brim with a double row of backstitches and turn the hat inside out.

Reversible Floppy Hat

What's better than one hat? Two, of course! The way to have two hats in one is to make two floppy hats and sew them together at the brim. Presto, a reversible hat!

Materials:

two fabrics, ½ yard each
elastic, 1 inch wide, and long enough to
fit around your head twice
bias tape, as long as the elastic

How to Make It:

1. Follow Steps 1 through 6 for the Floppy Hat in the preceding project.
2. Turn both hats so that the right sides face out and the elastic casings are no longer visible. Fit one hat inside the other. The elastics should line up with each other. Try the hat on again to be sure it fits. You can still make changes in the width of the elastic.
3. Sew down the edges of each fabric; then pin the edges of the two hats together.
4. Carefully sew the brims together with two rows of small backstitches.

Headband Cover

If you have an extra piece of fabric from a dress that was shortened or made by hand, a matching headband is a nifty fashion accessory. You'll want to make several different-colored covers to go with all sorts of outfits.

Materials:
plastic headband
fabric strip, 1½ by 16 inches

How to Make It:
1. Sew down the raw edges at each end of the fabric.
2. Fold the fabric in half lengthwise, with right sides facing each other. Slip the plastic band into the crease. Pin it in, allowing just enough room for the band to slip back and forth.
3. Remove the plastic band. Sew together the sides and one end of the material with backstitches. Use the headband to push the material through the opening at the end so that the cover will be on the band.
4. Sew two small pieces of Velcro or two snaps inside the open end so that you can remove the plastic band.

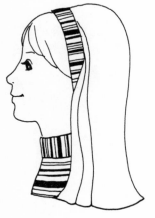

All-Purpose Skinny Band

Have you heard of cats with nine lives? This skinny band can lead at least that many. Wear it as a headband, an Indian band tied at your neck, or as a belt at either your waist or hips. Try tying it into a bow with long streaming ends and pin it to the back of your hair for special occasions.

Materials:
fabric, 3 to 4 inches wide by 40 inches long

How to Make It:
1. Fold fabric in half lengthwise, right sides facing each other.
2. Pin and sew it with backstitches, leaving one end open.
3. Turn it right-side out, using a long stick to push the cloth through.
4. Sew the ends together with small overhand stitches.

Three-Way Kerchief

The center slit makes this much more than just a kerchief to tie around your head.

Materials:
lightweight fabric, 30 inches square

How to Make It:
1. Cut the square into two triangles and sew down all the raw edges with backstitches or hemstitches.
2. Pin the two triangles together, along one side, with the right sides facing each other. Leave a 10 to 12 inch opening for your head.
3. Test to see if your head fits. Then sew it with backstitches.

Wear your kerchief folded into a triangle and tied under the chin. Slip it over your head to wear as a shawl. Holding the kerchief so that the opening is vertical, slip your head through the slit and tie the two points across the back for an elegant scarf hood.

For a gift, use two different-colored squares of fabric. Put different-colored triangles together and you will have two 2-toned scarves.

If you use a 36 inch square of a heavier fabric, your kerchief will become a poncho. Cut 8 inch lengths of wool; fold them in half; and sew them around the edges for fringes.

All Sorts of Bags

One-Piece Drawstring Bag

Drawstring bags are as useful as they are easy to make. Small versions can be used to hold combs, tissue, change, or jacks. Large bags, in sturdy sailcloth, might serve as fold-up duffle bags.

Materials:
fabric, 9 by 22 inches
drawstring rope or ribbon, 43 inches long

How to Make It:
1. With the wrong side of the fabric facing you, make a 1 inch casing on one 22 inch side of the fabric.
2. Make a slit into the center of the casing.
3. Fold side AB to meet side CD (see diagram). Sew both the side and the bottom with backstitches. Leave the casing unsewn. Turn the bag right side out.
4. Pull the drawstring through the casing with a safety pin, and tie the two ends together to make a handle.

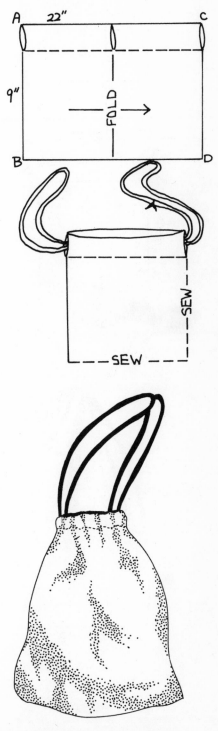

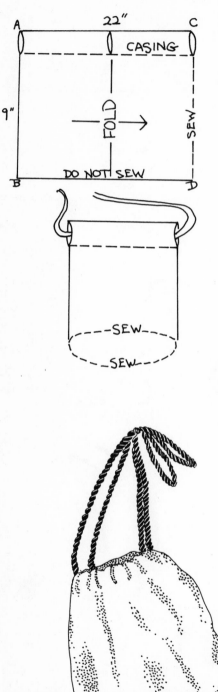

Round-Bottomed Drawstring Bag

Here's a roomier variation of the One-Piece Drawstring Bag. Make it in one color, or contrast the body of the bag with a different material at the bottom.

Materials:
⅛ yard fabric
drawstring rope or ribbon, 43 inches

How to Make It:
1. Cut a circle, using a 6 inch diameter plate as a template.
2. Cut a rectangle, 22 by 9 inches to fit around the circular base.
3. Follow Steps 2 and 3 for the One-Piece Drawstring Bag in the preceding project, but do not close the bottom.
4. Place the circular fabric with its right side against your working surface. Pin the body of the bag to the circle, with the wrong side of the fabric facing you. Now sew the bottom edge of the bag to the circle of cloth with backstitches.
5. Turn the bag inside out and pull through the drawstring handles.

Pants-Top Shoulder-Strap Bag

If you've got a pair of pants that have gotten too short or too tight, or have frayed bottoms, why not turn them into a go-everywhere shoulder-strap bag?

Materials:

one pair of high-waisted pants with good
    front detailing, such as patch pockets
zipper, the length of the pants' waist

How to Make It:

1. Cut off pants legs at the crotch.

2. Turn the pants top inside out and sew bottom seams with a backstitch.

3. Sew a zipper to the top and turn the bag right-side out again.

4. Use one of the cut-off pants legs for a shoulder strap. First cut off the seams and sew down the raw edges. Fold the fabric with the right sides facing each other so that the sewn-down edges meet (see diagram). Sew the edges together with a backstitch.

5. Tuck in the ends of your handle and sew with a running stitch. Sew each end of the handle on at opposite sides of the outside of the bag.

6. If your bag has no front patch pockets, remove pockets from another garment and sew those on instead. Decorative details can be added with stitching, appliques, or other trims.

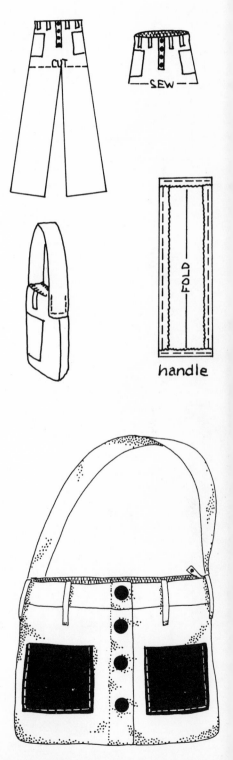

handle

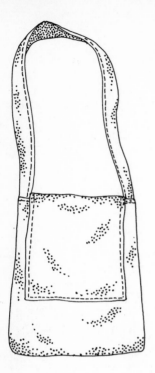

Pants-Leg Bag

Sometimes the top of a pair of pants wears out before the legs. Save the legs and the waistband and make yourself another useful bag.

Materials:
slacks, preferably with bell bottoms

How to Make It:
1. Cut the pants legs off just below the knee. Cut halfway down each seam of this leg and cut off the front portion. This piece will be about 6 inches long. The back part of the leg will remain as a flap closing.
2. Turn the bag inside out and sew the bottom edges together with a backstitch.
3. Tuck and pin all the raw edges around the flap and opening of the bag, and sew them down with a hemstitch.
4. For the handle, cut the waistband off the pants. Sew each end to the inside of the bag with backstitches. You can also use a ribbon handle. Whatever kind of handle you use, be sure to sew it on firmly since it takes a lot of pulling and must be secure.
5. Turn the bag right-side out and make a snap or button-and-loop closing if you want. This is optional.
6. The bag can be decorated.

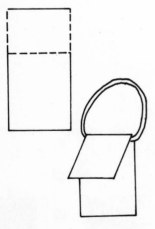

Kangaroo-Pocket Bag

A wide shoulder strap goes all around this bag, making it roomy. The extra pocket in front is handy for keys and change. For a high-fashion look, combine two textures of fabric. The illustrated bag was made from corduroy and a stretchy acrylic print.

Materials:

fabric, 8 by 26 inches for the body of the bag; ¼ yard by 60 inches for the handle and the outside pocket (if fabric is less than 60 inches wide, you will have to piece together the handle)

How to Make It:

1. Fold the 8 by 26 inch material in half the long way. Cut through the crease so that you have two pieces of cloth, each measuring 8 by 13 inches.

2. Cut around the bottom of the material (the 8 inch side) so that each piece has one rounded end, as shown in the sketch.

3. Cut a piece of cloth measuring 6½ by 13 inches from the second piece of fabric. Fold it in half and cut around the edges of your fabric, as you did in Step 2, so that both ends are rounded. This will be the outside pocket.

4. Refold the pocket so that the right sides are together and sew the cut edges together with a backstitch. Leave a 4 to 5 inch opening. Turn the pocket right-side

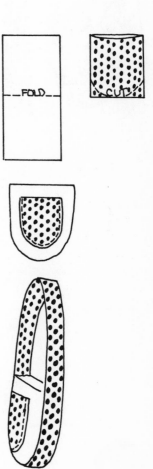

out through the opening. Fold in the edges of the opening and sew them together with overhand stitches.

5. Pin the pocket to one of the body pieces of the bag and sew it on with backstitches.

6. To make the handle, cut a piece of fabric 7 by 60 inches. Fold over and sew down the raw edges. Then fold the handle in half lengthwise and sew the two sides together with a backstitch.

7. Sew the two 7 inch ends of the handle together with a backstitch.

8. Pin the handle to the sides of the bag so that the handle seams are at the bottom. Now sew them together with backstitches.

Pretty-Face Pajama Bag

This gay bag holds everything you need to take to a slumber party. Keep it on your bed, or hang it on a hook. Make a few extras in different shapes and stuff them with shredded old nylons or bits of foam, for a whole "wardrobe" of throw pillows.

Materials:
fabric, ½ yard
zipper, 7 to 9 inches
wool, buttons, bits of lace and felt

How to Make It:
1. Use a large plate as a template (14 inch diameter is fine) and cut two circles of fabric.
2. Pin the circles together, with the right sides of the fabric together. Sew the two circles of fabric together with back-stitches, leaving a 7 or 9 inch opening for the zipper.
3. Sew the zipper in place, and turn the bag right-side out.
4. Decorate the bag. The illustrated bag was decorated with a braid made by divid-ing long strands of wool into three sec-tions and braiding as you would hair. The braid was pinned around the pillow, with the ends swinging loosely. A center por-tion of the braid was left loose to be used later as a handle or loop for hanging. The braid was sewn in place with small over-

hand stitches. Two pieces of lace were sewn on for eyes, with dark felt for pupils. Eyes can also be made out of buttons. A bit of red felt is a mouth. The felt can be glued or sewn. A small button was used for a nose.

With a bit of imagination you can use all kinds of odds and ends to create interesting and amusing faces for your pajama bag.

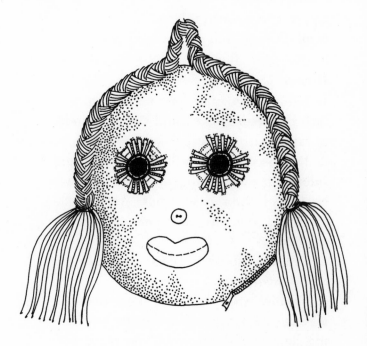

Tennis-Racket Bag

A carrier for your tennis racket can be made almost exactly like the pajama bag.

Materials:
fabric, ½ yard sturdy fabric, such as denim, sailcloth, or quilted cotton
zipper, 11 or 12 inches long, or very heavy snaps

How to Make It:
1. Use your tennis racket as a template and make a paper pattern by tracing the racket and two inches of the handle on a double layer of newspaper. Since you will need room for the rim of the tennis racket, draw a freehand outline beyond the one you made. This should extend about ½ an inch from the original line. Staple the newspaper pattern together and make sure it fits the racket.
2. Cut two pieces of fabric to match the paper pattern.
3. Pin the fabric together, with the right sides facing each other, leaving the portion where the zipper will go unpinned. Sew the two pieces of cloth together with backstitches. Try the cover on the racket before pinning and sewing the zipper.
4. Sew in the zipper and turn the cover right-side out again.
5. Decorate as you did the pajama bag.

Initials; little appliques of tennis rackets and insignia; tennis terms, like "love"; rick-rack; or ball-fringe trims would all make for a colorful and original carrier.

If you prefer, you can use heavy snaps instead of a zipper. Snaps made with an automatic snapmaker are very sturdy. These handy gadgets are available in all notions and hardware stores, and the cost is very low.

To make a carrier for your tennis balls, make yourself a small drawstring bag. Use a piece of fabric 6 by 12 inches and follow the directions for the One-Piece Drawstring Bag (see Contents). You can tie the drawstrings to the top of the racket handle. When you're playing, keep the bag inside the racket cover.

GUITAR CARRIER

If you don't play tennis, but do play a guitar, follow the same procedure to make a guitar carrier. However, the guitar is deeper than the tennis racket, and you must enlarge the basic outline by the depth of the instrument. You will have to use snaps for the instrument cover, since you probably wouldn't find a zipper large enough to close it.

Terry-Towel Laundry Bag

No more scattered socks and things after this laundry bag hangs at the back of a door or on a wall hook in your room.

Materials:
one wooden pants hanger
two towels of the same size
embroidery wool

How to Make It:
1. Pin towels together, right-sides out. Sew the sides, top, and bottom with very firm blanket stitches, leaving a 1 inch opening at the top of each side for the hanger bar to go through.
2. Cut an 8 to 10 inch slit into one towel. The slit should be 3 inches below the hanger casing.
3. Pin ribbon or bias tape all around the opening slit and sew down with backstitches.
4. Decorate with any type of embroidery decoration. If you like, you can add colorful appliques, either ready made or of your own design.

You can substitute a pillowcase for the towels. In that case, close the open side. Make a 2 inch casing for the pants-hanger bar. Slit as you would the terry-towel bag. If you use a solid-colored fabric, decorate it with waterproof magic markers. If you use a print, stitch

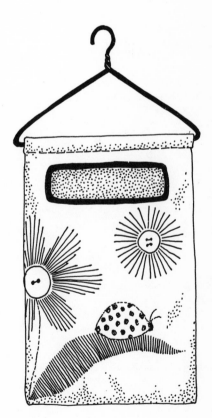

some of the lines in the print with embroidery threads. Don't be pennywise and pound foolish by using an old and very worn case that will wear out quickly when it is stuffed with lots of dirty clothes.

Lined Tote Bag

Make this bag with a very sturdy fabric. Upholstery fabric is especially good. If there are any old heavy winter coats in your "throwaway" boxes, the backs can be cut out. These totes make great school-book carriers or shopping bags.

Materials:

1 yard of fabric for the outside of the bag;
   1 yard of fabric for the lining
heavy cord, about 36 inches

How to Make It:

1. Cut both fabrics into 17 by 36 inch pieces.
2. Pin the tote bag and the lining fabrics together with the right sides facing each other, leaving a 10 inch opening. Sew all edges together, except this opening, with backstitches. Turn the material right-side out and close the opening with overhand stitches.
3. Lay the material with the lining against your work surface. Fold it in half and sew the two sides together with backstitches. Then turn it right-side out.
4. Sew a strong decorative cord to each side of the bag, leaving a few inches loose at the bottom on each side, like a tassel.

A handle can be made from leftover fabric. Cut the fabric into a piece 4 by 22

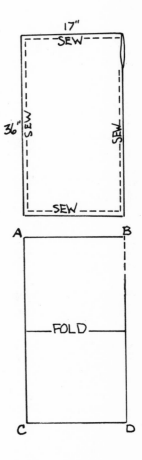

inches. Fold it in half, with the right sides together, and close all but a 2 inch opening. Turn it right-side out; close the opening; and sew each end of the handle to an inside seam of the bag. Now your bag is ready to be put to a variety of uses.

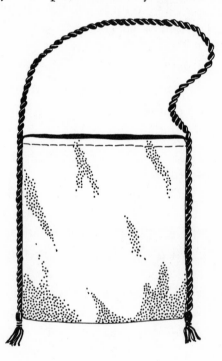

Jewelry

Stitch-and-Glue Bib Necklace

If you like Mexican jewelry, try colorful burlap glued to a cardboard base. A stitched casing holds a drawstring or chain, and a fringed bottom completes the look. Make it in one shade or mix your colors. Any way at all, it will be a compliment catcher.

Materials:

burlap, six 4 by 6 inch pieces
cardboard
1 yard decorative cord, or an 18 inch necklace chain

How to Make It:

1. Cut three pieces of cardboard to match Pattern 1, and one piece to match Pattern 2 (see page 62). Pattern 1 is the cardboard you will actually use to back your fabric. Pattern 2 is a guide for cutting the fabric. It is large enough to allow you to tuck in the edges and to make the casing on top and fringes at the bottom.

2. Cut three pieces of burlap to match Pattern 2.

3. Lay cardboard Pattern 1 against a cut piece of burlap. The fabric should extend an inch beyond the top and two inches

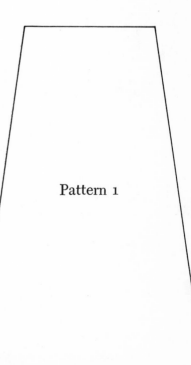

Pattern 1

beyond the bottom of the pattern. Fold over the sides and crease the burlap so that the cardboard and the fabric will be even at the sides.

4. Remove the cardboard and spread glue all over one side of it. Then press the fabric, with the edges of each side

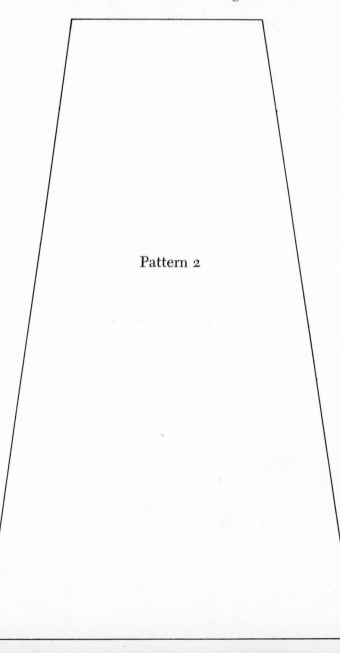

Pattern 2

tucked in, against the glued cardboard. Smooth it down with the back of a spoon or a small rolling pin. Glue down the creased edge of the casing.

5. Unravel the thread at the bottom, one thread at a time. Do this until the fringe touches the edge of the cardboard.

6. Cut burlap for the back of the cardboard (allow ½ inch all around, to tuck under the edges), and glue it in place.

7. Repeat steps 3, 4, and 5 for the other two pieces that make up the necklace.

8. Fold down the top casing, sew it in place with small hemstitches, and work the drawstring or necklace into the casing.

Decorative touches are optional, since burlap comes in an array of bright colors and looks great without additional ornaments. You can glue felt or embroidered appliques to each of the large pieces, or even decorate them with paint. The illustrated necklace was made of canary-yellow burlap, strung with orange twill and decorated with a bright-orange dot of acrylic paint on each piece.

9. Protect burlap against dirt with several coats of clear plastic spray or fabric protector.

The bib is only one way you can use this stitch-and-glue technique. You can make single pendants of various shapes. You can make the bib in one large piece, or make more, but smaller, pieces and wear an Egyptian collar.

Stitch-and-Glue Drop Earrings

Here is a stunning pair of earrings to match your bib necklace.

Materials:
burlap scraps, two colors
cardboard
drop-earring findings

How to Make It:
1. Make cardboard patterns as you did for the Stitch-and-Glue Bib Necklace in the preceding project, but reduce the size by one third.
2. Cut four pieces of burlap, two of each color. Since earrings swing freely, it will be fun to have a different color for the front and back of each earring.
3. Follow the directions for the bib necklace, but omit the casing. Instead, sew an earring finding to the center of each earring with small overhand stitches. Your needle will go through the fabric but need not go through the cardboard. (See Sources of Supplies for earring findings.)

Earrings can be made with other geometric shapes. Triangles and hexagons are very attractive.

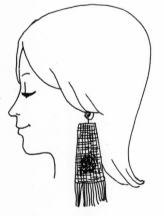

Reversible Pendant

A little fabric and decorative cord, and lots of imagination are all you need to create one-of-a-kind pendants.

Materials:

two 4 inch squares of fabric, either prints or solids
1 yard of decorative cord
necklace chain, or 24 inches of decorative cord
two 2½ inch plastic curtain rings or jump rings (jewelry findings)

How to Make It:

1. Pin the squares with the right sides together and sew them with backstitches.
2. With embroidery scissors cut out a square or circular opening, leaving a fabric frame of about ¾ of an inch all around (see sketch).
3. Turn the pendant inside out. If you wish, you can fill with very light stuffing of cotton or shredded old nylons. Sew all around the inside raw edge with blanket stitches, as shown in the illustration.
4. Twist the decorative cord into a string design having several edges touching the blanket-stitched edge of the frame. The illustrated pendant was decorated with cord twisted into three little figures to represent brotherhood. Sew the rope design in several spots with small overhand

stitches so that it will hold. Sew the parts that touch to the frame.

5. Sew a small ring to each end of the square and run a necklace chain or rope through this.

If you make a string design that would look best with the pendant hung at a corner, you will need only one ring.

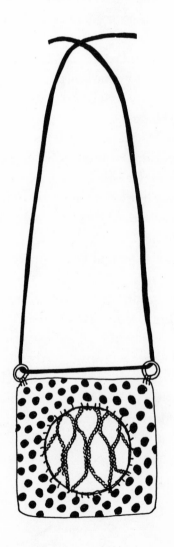

Adjustable Ring

It takes seconds to make these rings. They would make fine gifts at any time. Use them as Christmas-stocking stuffers.

Materials:

felt, ½ inch by 4 inches
embroidered patch, ½ to 1 inch
two ½ inch plastic curtain rings or gold
    jewelry jump rings (see jewelry findings)

How to Make It:

1. Sew the patch to the center of the felt strip, using small overhand stitches.
2. Pull one end of the felt through the two rings, as shown in the sketch. Bring the end around to the underside of the ring. Sew down with small hemstitches.
3. To wear, pull the unstitched end of the ring underneath the two loops. Bring around the top of the rings and tuck in between, adjusting to fit finger size.

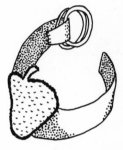

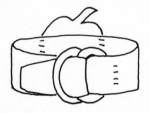

Embroidered Bracelet

Here's a wonderful way to use short pieces of ribbon. Velvet is especially lovely.

Materials:

velvet or other ribbon, 2 inches wide and long enough to fit your wrist plus ½ an inch so that raw edges can be tucked in

embroidered appliques, beads, buttons, or other trims

three snap closings or a 2 inch Velcro closing

How to Make It:

1. Sew down the raw edges at both ends of the bracelet.

2. Sew on decorations.

3. Sew a piece of Velcro to the inside of one end and another to the outside of the other end; or sew on snaps.

A 3 inch width of ribbon made like the bracelet would also make a handsome napkin ring. You might consider making a whole set for Mother's Day. No Velcro closing is needed for the napkin ring. Just sew the ends together.

Ribbon Choker

A ribbon choker is made the same way as the Embroidered Bracelet in the preceding project. However, 1 inch should be the maximum width of the choker, for a more graceful look.

Materials:

¾ inch grosgrain ribbon, approximately
    12 inches long
    decorative trims
two jewelry clamps (see Sources of Supplies)
decorative cord

How to Make It:

1. Sew on the trimming.
2. Tuck under the raw edges at the ends and baste with a few running stitches. Press a clamp over each end.
3. Attach a length of decorative cord to the clamp loops. Use cords long enough so that the choker can do double duty as a headband.

Fabric Choker

Accessory variations you can create with this easy-to-make fabric choker are practically limitless. Fit it around your head. Lengthen it and use it as a belt. Make it from a sturdy fabric and put it around your dog's neck. Then you will understand why this type of choker is often called a dog collar.

Materials:

fabric, 2½ inches wide, and long enough to go around your neck, plus a ½ inch allowance so that raw edges can be sewn down

trimmings

½ to 1 inch piece of Velcro, or hooks and eyes

How to Make It:

1. Sew down the raw edges at the ends, and fold the fabric in half lengthwise, with the right sides facing each other. Sew down with backstitches, leaving one end open.

2. Turn it right-side out, using a pencil or a thin stick to push the fabric through. Close the opening with overhand stitches.

3. Sew on decorative trims.

4. Sew Velcro or a hook and eye to each end.

Super-Sized Finger/Scarf Ring

Here's a ring for anyone who likes to wear something chunky on her finger. The ring bands are adjustable, which makes them perfect as either rings or scarf holders.

Materials:
large, adjustable flat-topped ring (available from jewelry suppliers)
felt scraps
decorations

How to Make It:
1. Cut a ¾ inch circle of cardboard and a 1 inch circle of felt. Glue the cardboard circle to the center of the felt circle.
2. Cut a 1½ inch circle of felt. Sew on decorative stitches or an applique.
3. Stitch the decorated felt circle around the felt-and-cardboard base with small overhand stitches. When only a small opening is left, stuff a small amount of cotton inside so that the ring is shaped like a small pillow. Finish sewing all around.
4. Glue the flat felt bottom to the ring base.

There are many variations of ring bases. Some come with raised rims. If you use this type of ring, you must cut your ring fabric so that it will fit exactly inside this rim. If the ring is an oval, then you must cut your shapes oval rather than round.

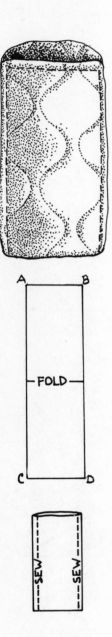

Gifts 'n' Things

Eyeglass Case

Keep your lenses scratch-free in a brightly colored case. Quilted fabric would be especially suitable. Consider this little case for a Father's Day gift, too, either as an eyeglass case or as a pipe holder.

Materials:
two pieces of fabric, 3 by 12 inches

How to Make It:
1. Sew down the raw edges at the sides of the material and pin the two pieces together, with the right sides facing each other. If you are not using quilted fabric, work a layer of cotton padding between the pinned pieces.
2. Sew fabric with backstitches, leaving an end open. Turn right-side out through the opening and close the open end.
3. Fold the sewn-together fabric in half so that sides CD meet sides AB, as shown in the diagram. Sew up the sides.

If you make a pipe holder, instead of folding the fabric in half, as you did in Step 3, fold it so that there is a 1 inch flap at the top, for the pipe head.

Pen or Pencil Holder

This is a variation of the Eyeglass Case. You don't need quilting or padding, since pencils and pens are less fragile than glasses.

Materials:
two pieces of fabric, 6 by 12 inches.

How to Make It:
1. Repeat the directions for the Eyeglass Case in the preceding project.
2. Make rows of stitches along the length of the pocket. For a combination eyeglass case with pencil holder, omit the row of stitching. Instead stitch two or three loops of fabric to the center of the eyeglass case.

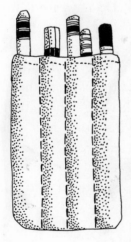

Wallet

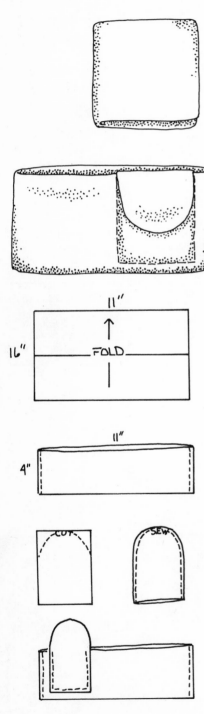

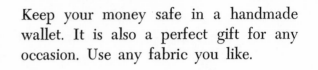

Keep your money safe in a handmade wallet. It is also a perfect gift for any occasion. Use any fabric you like.

Materials:
fabric, one piece 16 by 11 inches, two 4 by 7 inches
snaps or Velcro

How to Make It:
1. Fold 16 by 11 inch fabric in half lengthwise, with the right sides together. Sew the edges of two sides together. Turn inside out, and sew the third side. You will have a piece measuring 8 by 11 inches.
2. Fold the wallet in half again, so that it measures 11 by 4 inches. Close the two 4 inch sides. Do not turn it inside out yet.
3. To make the change purse, place the two 7 by 4 inch pieces together, with the right sides facing each other. Round off the top. Sew the sides of the change purse together, leaving the straight bottom open. Turn the purse inside out and close the straight edge.
4. Sew the purse to one side of the wallet, as shown in the sketch, and turn the wallet inside out.
5. Sew on snaps or Velcro to close the change purse. You can also sew on snaps or Velcro to close the wallet when it is folded in half, but this is not necessary.

Book Carrier With Bookmark

Protect your favorite book with a handy and handsome carrying case. The size can be adjusted.

Materials:

fabric, ⅝ yard for a 9½ by 14½ inch book

How to Make It:

1. Cut one piece of fabric 12 by 16 inches for the cover, two pieces 12 by 4½ inches for the inside flaps, and two pieces 2½ by 14 inches for the handles.

2. Sew down the raw edges at the top and bottom of the book cover (Sides AB and CD in diagram). Also sew down the raw edges of the handle pieces.

3. Fold the handles in half lengthwise with the right sides out. Sew edges together with overhand stitches.

4. Sew down the raw edge at one side of the flaps (FH in the diagram).

5. Pin the flaps to the sides of the cover, with the right sides facing each other. Pin handles between the flaps and the cover, and sew them down with backstitches.

6. Sew a decorative cord or ribbon to the inside center of your cover, where it folds. The cord should be the length of the page. Sew an embroidered or handmade patch to the end of the ribbon or cord.

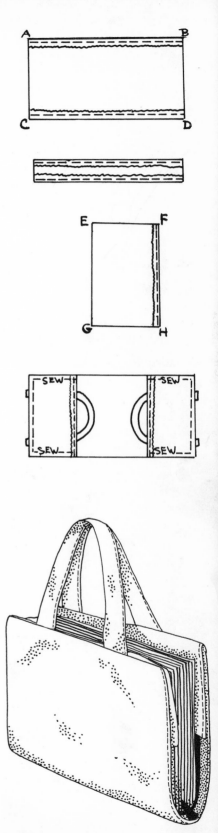

Button-on Collar and Cuffs

Wear a button-on collar as you would a necklace, to brighten the neckline of a dress, blouse, or sweater. Complete the look with matching button-on cuffs.

Materials:

two pieces of fabric, 4 by 14 inches for the collar; four pieces, 4 inches wide and long enough to go around your wrist plus 1 inch for tucking down, for a pair of cuffs. If you use felt you need only half the amount of fabric, since you will be working with a single layer
decorative thread, beads, trimmings
two 9 inch paper plates

How to Make It:

1. Cut a slit into the rim of a paper plate and cut away the center of the plate. Try the paper collar around your neck. Bend the edges back at an angle until it fits snugly. Cut away excess paper.
2. Cut the collar fabric ½ inch larger than the paper pattern.
3. Baste the raw edges on the collar pieces and sew them together, with the right sides facing each other. Leave a 2 inch opening, so that the collar can be turned right-side out. Close the open end when it is turned.
4. With embroidery thread stitch around

the collar with blanket stitches. Sew on other decorations.

5. Sew a decorative button or bead from an old necklace at one end of the collar. Make a loop from the embroidery wool and sew it to the other end. If you use a bead or pearl closing, sew some beads or pearls around the edges of the collar. Use embroidery thread to stitch your initials on the edge of the collar.

If you like, scallop the edge of your collar instead of following the outline of the plate.

Make the cuffs like the collar, but first cut the paper pattern in half to fit snugly around your wrist.

Portable Sewing Kit

These nifty travel accessories hold enough needles and thread to take care of emergencies. They are welcome gifts for almost any occasion.

Materials:

½ yard of 2 inch wide ribbon
lightweight fabric, such as muslin or interfacing, ½ inch by 14 inches
pins, needles, several colors of thread wrapped around cardboard, and other sewing supplies

How to Make It:

1. Sew down the raw edges at each end of the ribbon.
2. Cut around the lightweight material with pinking shears. Pin on pins, needles, and thread wrapped around bits of cardboard.
3. Place the fabric with the sewing equipment face up against the inside of the ribbon. There should be a ribbon border all around. Sew down the fabric holding the equipment at sides A and B (see diagram). Do not sew down sides C and D; just tack it with a stitch here and there. If you do not leave Sides C and D loose you will not be able to replace sewing things as they are used up, without pinning through to the outside of the ribbon.

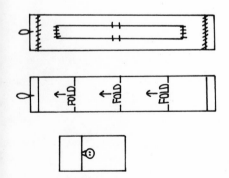

4. Fold the sewing case like a wallet. Sew a loop to the closing edge of the ribbon, and a button to the other side to keep the portable sewing kit closed when it is not in use.

5. Press the case well so that the folds will stay in place.

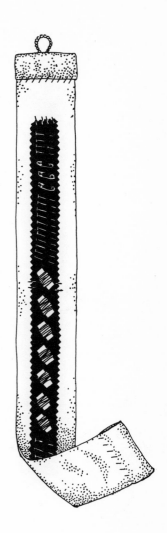

Fingernail Gloves

Here is an opportunity to express your sense of humor: make gloves with whimsical printed "fingernails."

Materials:
one pair solid-colored cotton gloves
printed fabric scraps

How to Make It:
1. Cut out ten fabric fingernails.
2. Sew down the raw edges.
3. Pin the fingernails to the tops of the glove fingers and sew them down with small hemstitches. To avoid sewing the fingers together, slip the end of a spoon into each finger as you pin and sew.

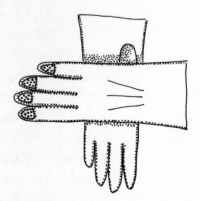

Slipper Sox

Use these as both Christmas stockings and gifts. They will look great filled with candy and hanging over the mantle. They will feel cozy on a cold winter day.

Materials:
one pair of socks
felt, ⅓ yard

How to Make It:
1. Place your foot or the foot of the person for whom you are making the socks on a piece of white paper or newspaper. Draw a pattern around the foot. Repeat this for the other foot. If you're making a surprise gift, use a pair of shoes.
2. Following an outline of the foot somewhat larger than your pencil line, cut two pieces of felt.
3. Stitch the felt all around the bottom of each sock with embroidery wool, using a blanket stitch.
4. Cut decorative shapes from the leftover felt and sew them on the front of the sock. You can also decorate with embroidery stitches, appliques, beads, and so forth. If you're a skier, this is a great way to use some of the ski patches skiers collect.

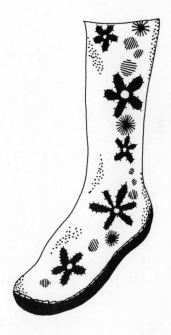

Room Accessories

Mini/Maxi-Frog Pillow

Tiny stuffed animal pillows are fun to stand on a knickknack shelf. They're useful, too, as pincushions. Larger stuffed animals make amusing and decorative throw pillows.

Materials:
two pieces of fabric, 4 by 8 inches
shredded nylon, foam, or cotton
buttons, embroidery wool, or other trims

How to Make It:
1. Make a sketch of the frog on a piece of newspaper, using the illustration as a guide, and cut two pieces of fabric from the pattern.
2. Sew buttons where the frog's eyes will go, and embroider decorations on the frog's body.
3. Pin the two pieces together, with the right sides facing each other, leaving an opening. Sew with backstitches and turn right-side out.
4. Push stuffing through the opening, making the back of the frog plump. Sew the open section with small overhand stitches.

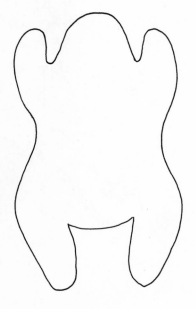

You'll want to make pigs, monkeys, Humpty-Dumptys, and all sorts of animals and figures this way. You'll also want to enlarge the frog pattern (or any others you design) for some wonderful maxi-pillows to dress up a bed or a sofa. A third of a yard of fabric will be sufficient to make a maxi-frog pillow measuring approximately 10 by 14 inches. Use different kinds of fabric for the bottoms and tops so that you can make use of scraps. Except for cutting a larger pattern, the maxi-pillow is made exactly the same way as the mini-pillow.

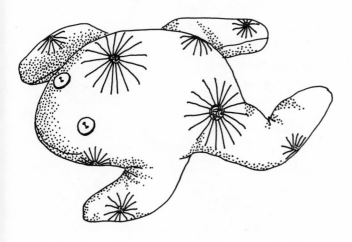

Hanging Room-Organizer

It's easier to keep a room orderly when there's a place for everything. This neat pocketed organizer will hold notebooks, pencils, pens, art supplies, and stationery.

Materials:
½ yard of sturdy fabric, such as denim chain or pants hanger

How to Make It:
1. Cut a 14 by 34 inch rectangle, and sew down the raw edges at the bottom and sides with backstitches.
2. Make a 1 inch casing at the top.
3. Cut three 10 inch squares out of the remaining fabric (or use a contrasting print for a more cheerful look). Use a plate as a template to round out the bottoms of the squares for better-looking pockets.
4. Sew down the raw edges and then sew the pockets to the denim.
5. Divide the pockets into compartments by making backstitches down the centers. Additional small pockets can be stitched to the tops of the pockets. These will hold smaller items.
6. Slip a pants hanger or a chain into the casing. If you use a decorative chunky chain, you can slip the organizer around your neck and actually wear it and use it

as an apron (in that case, sew some ribbons to each side and tie it around your waist). The organizer can also be used as a shower caddy for shampoo, cosmetics, and other personal items for summer camp.

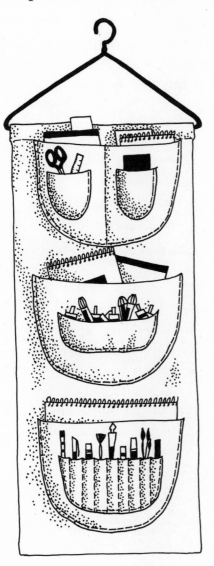

Photo Banner

Here's a different sort of banner. Its open pockets permit you to slide photographs in and out.

Materials:

sturdy fabric, like sailcloth or upholstery fabric

one or two felt squares

How to Make It:

1. Cut the material into a triangle measuring 12 by 18 by 18 inches. Sew down the raw edges.

2. Cut twelve ½ inch wide strips of felt: six 3¾ inches long and six 2¾ inches long. Place these strips as frames for snapshots onto your banner. Backstitch three sides of the frames, but merely tack down the edges of the fourth side so that you can slip snapshots in and out.

The sizes of the frames can be adjusted for photographs of different sizes. The banner can be made larger also.

3. Cut 2 by 4 inch loops from felt or ribbons and sew them to the top of the banner. Push a thin dowel or chain through the loops to hang your banner.

Mirror-Eyed-Kitten Flower Holder

The mirror eyes of this kitten won't take the place of a full-length mirror, but they will add a bright and sparkling peek-a-boo decoration to your wall. A small pocket in back, sewn between the kitten's ears, can serve as a container for dried flowers or as a secret pocket for notes and small items.

Materials:
large scrap of sturdy upholstery fabric or felt (about 12 by 12 inches)
two small oval mirrors
embroidery yarn
three or four 12 inch pipe cleaners
two ½ inch curtain rings

How to Make It:
1. Draw a picture of a kitten's head on a piece of paper. Make it no larger than 9 by 12 inches. You can use a coloring-book picture as a model.
2. Cut the fabric, following the paper pattern.
3. Mark the spots where the mirror eyes will go with chalk or tailor's chalk, and embroider the outline with large overhand stitches. Use these same stitches or a blanket stitch to outline the entire cat.
4. Sew the cat's pipe-cleaner whiskers in place with black or brown embroidery

thread. Add a little stitched triangle above the whiskers for the cat's nose, or sew on a small dark button.

5. Glue the mirror eyes in place.

6. Cut a pocket out of cloth scraps to fit between the cat's eyes. Sew this in place at three sides, leaving the top open.

7. Sew a curtain ring to the top of each ear. Use the rings to hang up the cat. Fill the pockets with some dried flowers or weeds and you'll have the most talked-about room accessory ever.

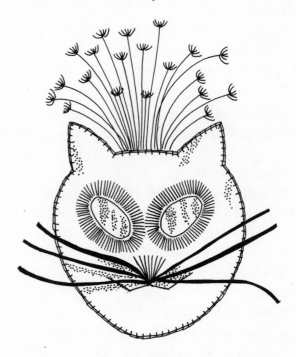

Fish Mobile

When your friends see these fish gently swaying on their strings, they'll want to know what they're made of. Watch their surprised looks when you say, "Powder puffs!"

Materials:

five or six powder puffs. Combine different shapes and sizes; 3 inch circles are ideal

two buttons for each fish

rickrack or other trimming string

dowel, hanger, or a large curtain ring from which to suspend mobile

How to Make It:

1. Place a button on each side of a powder puff, so that the buttons line up with each other. The buttons should be where the fish eyes would go. Sew them together.

2. To give your fish scales, wind rickrack or other narrow trim from the top, down around the back of the fish. Tack down with one or two stitches at the top or the bottom. You don't need to sew all the way around the fish.

3. Twist some of the decorative trim into a tail and sew it in place. You can also add some fins this way.

4. When the fish are decorated, string a needle with double duty thread. Make a double knot and pull the thread through the top of the fish. Tie the end of the string to your dowel, curtain hanger, or hanger. Repeat this until all your fish are hung.

You can turn powder puffs into other shapes and objects, too, of course. You can make all kinds of funny heads to represent different members of your family or your friends. Buttons, felt, and embroidery stitches would create features. Yellow, brown, and red wool can be used for hair.

Sources of Supplies

Most of the materials used to make the projects in this book can be found in fabric stores or the notions sections of department stores.

Those of you who like to shop by mail, can find sewing supplies and equipment (including tiny zippers and Velcro) pictured in a free 20-page illustrated catalogue. Write to:

Home-Sew, Inc.
1825 West Market St.
Bethlehem, Pa. 18018

Jewelry supplies are available in most hobby shops. Jewelart, Inc. fills small orders on any item described in the book. For a catalogue write to:

Jewelart, Inc.
7753 Densmore Avenue
Van Nuys, Calif. 91406

Index

⸻

About the Author

Joellen Sommer is a fifteen-year-old student at the Hewlett High School in Long Island.

Joellen learned to operate a sewing machine in junior high school, and two years ago saved enough money to buy her own machine. Since then she has been sewing for herself and for her mother as well. She enjoys making accessories because they are fast and easy to make and she can always find enough fabric for them.

Joellen lives with her mother, author of Lothrop's *The Bread Dough Craft Book,* her father, her older brother Paul, and Baggins, a Miniature Schnauzer with crooked teeth and a lovable personality.